Corporeal & Astral Manifestations of Good & Evil

by Henry Kirchhoff

Corporeal & Astral Manifestations of Good & Evil

Author: Henry Kirchhoff

Copyright © 2014 Psychoplasmic Pulp Publishing

ISBN: 9780692379974

Book I:
Corporeal, Psychic & Astral Planes

Astral Axioms

I. The planar hierarchy consists of five planes: the physical, the mental-emotional (psychic), the spiritual, the universal, and the one-realm. On each plane below the one realm there are manifestations of the four essences: good, evil, chaos, and order.

II. Man's perception is limited to the first two planes as humans are composed of the physical and the mental-emotional. On these two planes, man has several means of interpreting the world around them. These means are the senses in the physical plane and the emotions in the psychic plane.

III. Though we only perceive the first two planes, we are bound to each of the planes by the spiritual-social collective. Energy as information manifests in the spiritual-social collective as collective knowledge.

IV. Each individual is born composed of a balance of all four energies, but over time, we develop alignment with one of the essences. In the spiritual-social collective, each individual flows with one of the four essences.

V. The four essences are deviations from the central essence of the one realm. This central essence is composed of an equal balance of two sub-essences. From one of the sub-essences, chaos and order sprang, and from the other, good and evil sprang.

VI. If an individual's primary composition or alignment is with chaos or order, they are subject to a variable sub-alignment with either good or evil. Likewise, if an individual's primary composition or alignment is with good or evil, they are subject to a variable sub-alignment with either chaos or order.

The Planar Hierarchy

The Physical Realm

Mankind perceives his existence on the physical plane via the five senses: taste, touch, smell, hearing, and sight. Good and evil manifest as pleasure and pain respectively. The relationship between good and evil on the physical plane is synonymous with the survival paradigm in which life (perpetuated by pleasure) and death (signified by pain) exist at opposite ends of a spectrum that motivates our existence.

The Mental-Emotional (Psychic) Realm

Mankind perceives his existence on the mental-emotional plane via the five emotions: fear, anger, sadness, happiness, love. On the physical plane, each sense can be accessed to promote pleasure or discomfort. Something can taste sweet or bitter. However, while each sense on the physical plane exists with the potential to perpetuate both survival and death, emotions are delegated exclusively to either signifying increased chances of survival or death. For example, sadness serves as a signifier of unhappiness, a need for change in state.

If we are sad, we are moving down the survival scale. If we are happy, we are moving up the survival scale. But our conscience has to make the choice as to what to do with the emotional signifier. The senses compel us to do things. The smell of rotten food compels some people to vomit, or at least create a distance between oneself and the source of smell. The sight of a dead body makes us quiver, stumble, run, and possibly once again, vomit. We are compelled towards the survival mechanism on the physical plane. On the mental-emotional plane, we have the choice to react to survival indicators.

On the physical plane an animal eats a berry and it tastes bitter so he spits it out. On the mental-emotional plane, a person indulges in the fruits of emotional gratification, and guilt or sadness will be the only thing that compels the individual to spit out some perceived emotional gratification from their life. This is one of the downsides of the mental-emotional plane: we are granted free will, but we are not assisted by instinct, which compels us to avoid signifiers of death on the physical realm.

The Spiritual Realm

The manifestations of good and evil on the spiritual realm are sin and virtue. Mankind can only conceive of sin and virtue by utilizing all of his emotions and senses. What true virtue is then, is the moderation of all senses and emotions. Relating back to research in "Quantifying Chaos," the balance between the emotions and senses leads to a minimal perceptual chaos. A mental state of minimal perceptual chaos allows one to make efficient choices. The spiritual realm moderates the choices made in the mental-emotional realm, in that the spiritual framework limits our choice to an affiliation with either good or evil tendencies. We are always free to make decisions adverse to our prior spiritual disposition, but no matter what we choose, the compilation of our choices is qualified in terms of good and evil.

Mankind's understanding of sin and virtue is relative to the environment surrounding. While the physical and mental-emotional planes provide self-based perpetuation of survival and maintenance of well-being, the spiritual plane is where mankind as a collective spiritual unit begins to become apparent. The manifestation of this collective on the physical realm is society. The manifestation of this collective on the mental-emotional realm is collective social information. Collective social information is essentially a society's common knowledge, which in terms of tradition, political function, and education, tend to increase in a society the longer it exists.

Virtue in a social capacity is the perpetuation of good throughout a community or society. Virtue hinges upon an individual's empathy for others. There is both physical and mental-emotional empathy. Empathy assists in the moderation of senses and emotions in those surrounding a crisis, and compels them to spread this balance through the means they deem necessary. Empathy, after all, is truly painful to most human beings. It is through this associated pain that we develop distaste for violence.

The spiritual plane is the highest plane man currently exists in. We can generally only perceive our existence in the spiritual realm as a representational state in which the **spiritual social collective** manifests on the physical plane as society and on the mental-emotional plane as **social common knowledge**, which allows us to chart the spiritual composition of our society and the general spiritual state we exist in.

The Spiritual-Social Collective

As established above, the spiritual social collective manifests on the physical plane as society. The spiritual collective is composed of positive, negative, and neutral energies. Each independent energy system in the spiritual collective represents an individual in society. Positive and negative energy systems attract, whereas neutral energy systems provide a minor attraction towards either positive or negative.

We interpret the energies surrounding us using our energy composition.

Social bonds create local organizations of energy in the spiritual collective. Though friends may be distanced geographically on the physical plane, their independent energy systems can be near one another in the energy realm.

In addition, bonds in the spiritual collective can become established on the physical plane such as when two individuals have no knowledge of one another at all but share thoughts. This occurs when information being processed into social common knowledge is realized by two individuals at the same time. It is referred to as "100th Monkey Syndrome." The story begins with two scientists studying monkeys on two separate islands in the pacific. After months of waiting for social development, one of the monkeys washed their food, and the whole society followed suit. Then, a phenomenon unexplainable to this day occurred: the monkeys on the neighboring island, with no physical contact to those on the prior, started to wash their food as well.

The independent systems within the spiritual collective share bond through social collective knowledge.

The closer our personal realities and our social realities are, the more likely we are to elevate towards individuals we are bound to in the collective. But the more secrets we have, the more we deviate from our social or projected reality, the more likely we are to alienate ourselves from those near us on the physical plane, and draw independent systems of equal or greater sin in the spiritual collective. In such an instance, those independent systems composed primarily of sin share a bond of common knowledge reinforced by sin, which causes these people to elevate towards sin in both the mental-emotional and physical realms.

In order to ascend to the spiritual realm fully, man has to have good ethics and morals established, and he must be socially aware so as to facilitate the development of virtue. Then, the personal reality must coincide with the social reality to the greatest degree allowed by that individual's capacities. Those who do not sin will consequently have less to hide and less guilt. In addition, they will be less likely to create bonds via sinful collective knowledge, making them less prone to sin on the mental-emotional and physical planes.

A large reason that ascending to the spiritual realm has yet to be attained by many is because individuals don't understand why sin is of immediate consequence. Several religions argue against the immediate consequence of sin, emphasizing consequence after the fact, in eternal damnation, without any chance for reform.

A second reason spiritual ascendance hasn't occurred for most is because the religions of the world give mankind no blueprint for a means of gravitating towards virtue naturally. Rather, they teach us how to resist what we are inclined to do with the promise of eternal bliss after our diminishing lifespan the only incentive.

It is of utmost importance that mankind be imbued with a sense of immediate purpose when referring to virtue's function. Through ethical and moral development, man can understand goodness in a way that compels him to be virtuous, rather than a system of guilt and shame that compels him to not be sinful.

While the above factors play a large role in preventing mankind from ascending to the spiritual level, the primary reason mankind cannot fully merge with the spiritual realm is the dichotomous relationship between pleasure and virtue on the survival scale. In the physical realm, mankind perceives pleasure as a perpetuate of survival. In the spiritual realm, however, the conceptual existence of virtue leads man to the logical conclusion that pleasure is equated with sin and death, as most indulgence in pleasure is recognized as sin.

The Universal Realm

Only four primary energies or essences operate at the universal level: chaos, order, good, and evil. These four basic energies are the compilation of all energies from the lower planes. This is the level at which maintenance is crucial. It is at this level that imbalance of the cosmic forces will influence the lower planes.

The One Realm

Chaos, order, good and evil, and all other dichotomies, anti-theses, etc., exist as one here.

11

Laws of the Realms

The Planar Laws are a series of given constants within the planar system. These rules hold true for each of the realms, or involve each in some way.

The First Law of Realms: Each realm is less restricted by time and space as you progress up the planar scale. In the one-realm, all space and time is one. On the physical plane, perception of space is relative to location and time is segregated into past, present, and future. In the spiritual realm time and space are less restrictive.

The Second Law of Realms: Each plane below another is subject to the laws of the higher planes. For example, in the physical realm a being's perception of pleasure and pain is derived from the manifestations of this dichotomy on higher levels, those being: sin and virtue, good and evil, etc.

Likewise, the entities of each plane, conscious or non, influence the faculties of the higher, even if indiscernible to most. For example, when violence occurs in society, it is an indication of the composition of good and evil in the social collective, but also influences the social collective by changing the feelings of others.

The Third Law of Realms: Conception of planar phenomena, and our relationship to these phenomena on higher planes precedes actual ascendance to a new plane.

The Fourth Law of Realms: The universe becomes less distinct as we progress up the ladder.

The Fifth Law of Realms: Each plane has a cosmic function while simultaneously functioning to provide man the framework to spiritual ascendance. For example, the cosmic function of the physical realm is to incubate energy in closed environments (the body) so the energy may undergo conversion and re-immersion into the social and universal collectives.

The physical plane functions as a framework to spiritual ascendance in that it allows us to gain a sense of self in order to realize things exist separate of ourselves, which leads later to social awareness and the concept of virtue through empathy.

The Sixth Law of the Realms: The five realms are encompassed by planar vortices that function like an immaterial refracting fabric. The entities within each plane are reflections of the universal collective. Due to the planar vortices, the primary essences in the universal realm tend to become refracted increasingly as they move down the planar scale, as if each vortice is a prism, dividing the light of the one essence.

The Respective Social Compounds in an Autonomous System

Below the basic denominations are laid out. Added are the denominations of good and evil, additional denominations of chaos and order, and the respective roles individuals play in these denominations and independent of the denominations.

The Denominations of Chaos and Order

The Anarchist: The anarchist is the parent of neo-anarchy. The anarchist strives to create a system of the purest chaos possible without achieving equilibrium

The Order-Based: The order-based strive to achieve pure order at its greatest potential capacity. They want to stabilize chaotic systems and then replace them with a single order. Religious assimilation is an example of replacing chaotic individual systems with a single order.

The Neo-Anarchist: The Neo-Anarchist believes that the state of equilibrium at which pure order = pure chaos is desirable. The neo-anarchist believes that this equilibrium is the foundation for rebirth.

If we add an order to the state of autonomy it becomes a distinctive system, thus tipping the scales back towards a majority of chaos. If we try to make the system more chaotic, we are only perpetuating the autonomy, and ultimately, the equilibrium. The neo-anarchist both maintains the order of an autonomous system, and perpetuates chaos in an ordered system, should one arise to threaten autonomy.

Neo-anarchists do not senselessly destroy or wreak havoc. Neo-anarchists must calculate, and determine the most advantageous time to administer their reactions upon the world.

The Neutral: The neutral choose neutrality or elevate towards it through complacency and apathy.

The Denominations of Good and Evil

The Sinners

Sinners are grouped in two basic factions: those limited to only physical and mental-emotional capacities, thus selfish, and those who are aware of the spiritual forces in the world and intentionally or unintentionally spread evil. The sinners segregate as follows:

The Limited

The Self-Inflicting Sinners: The limited are generally harmless to those surrounding, save perhaps those who are in very close proximity on the physical and mental-emotional planes. That is to say that they have very little effect on the spiritual collective, save on their own independent system. The self-inflicting sinners include the gluttonous, lustful, the self-preserving, the greedy, the envious, and the apathetic.

The Malicious Sinners: killers, rapists, and those who perform other crimes against humanity through force, who are compelled by physical and mental-emotional motivations only. The malicious sinners do affect the spiritual collective; however, all of the manifestations of sin and evil they create in the spiritual collective are generally inadvertent.

15

The Ascendant

Hate-Breeders: The hate-breeder sin and are aware of the effects of sinning. They use the hatred in an individual to reinforce in said individual a synthetic limitation to only the physical and mental-emotional capacities. When an individual feels hatred consistently, especially towards another, he or she generally wishes to inflict harm on them through mental or emotional means. This limits those who hate to a perception of the survival scale in which pain leads us closer to death and pleasure to elongated life. These individuals are essentially robbed of virtue, as they are incapable of seeing that pain inflicted on another damages the collective and social networks.

In addition to using hate already inherit in an individual, the hate-breeder has the ability to produce hate in individuals as well.

Fear-Breeders: The fear-breeder augments paranoia in individuals. Fear is always guided by the notion that there is an aggressor and that the target will potentially become the victims. If fear is displaced, then it can cause distrust of, and withdrawal from, the social collective. By doing so, the fear-breeder has created in a potentially spiritual individual a synthetic state of self-preservation, in which withdrawal from society for the sake of survival results in a loss of notions of social obligation and virtue.

Breeders of Despair: The breeder of despair generates unhappiness in the world and in individuals by causing tragedy. The breeder of despair is marked by its isolation from others in the spiritual collective and relative closeness in the physical realm. The breeder of despair causes individuals to elevate towards its spiritual composition in the spiritual collective, augments despair in the physical realm, and then feeds off all of the resulting energies spread through common knowledge. The despair is left to resonate in the social collective, and is either dispersed through others or eventually leads to the physical and collective isolation of those in despair.

The Virtuous

The virtuous are the spiritually ascendant, or those who have developed a strong sense of empathy and moral ethics through reasoning and experience. The virtuous act as if the social unit is a single body. As with the sinners, there are the inadvertent virtuous and those who intentionally work to spread virtue throughout society.

The Limited

Those who are virtuous, caring, kind, empathetic to the greatest degree moral reasoning will allow, but are not conscious of the spiritual collective. Though they spread virtue, or at least are characterized by virtue, they do so through the physical and mental-emotional faculties, primarily, reasoning.

The Ascendant

Justice Seekers: Equivocated with the knight, the justice seekers hunt the ascendant sinners. Since the work of the virtuous ascendant is not totally antithetical to the work of the ascendant sinners, the justice seekers try to create a balance between the two, not by converting sin to virtue, but rather by destroying the potential weavers of sin.

The Romantic: The romantic has a natural affinity towards connecting people on the physical realm who share bonds in the spiritual collective. By doing so, the romantic brings the physical society closer to the spiritual collective. The spiritual collective is an autonomous system of spiritual pairings and segregation of will, by will, which, if paralleled in physical society, could potentially allow for an autonomous society.

The Conductor: The conductor orchestrates the societies and political systems in which the social collective can strive. Though the Greeks may not have ascribed to the belief of a spiritual collective, the philosophers were inclined to promote virtue in their political developments. The conductor, in this respect, may be promoting virtue without a sense of the spiritual collective, thus qualifying the conductor as inadvertent-virtuous. However, it is the role of the conductor to create frameworks from which virtuous societies can spring, and, through the ages conductors, primarily philosophers, kings, and politicians have become increasingly aware of the merits of virtue on a social and spiritual level.

The Distinctive Qualities of Man, Independent of Denominative Affiliation:

Psychic Vampires (negative and positive charge): Inextricably linked to the social collective. The strongest have the potential to link with world collective, possibly the universal collective. The social collective consists of positively charged individuals, negatively charged individuals, and neutral. The negatively charged give off the same energy when happy that a positive charged would when sad. The psychic vampire that is negatively aligned has a tendency to absorb byproduct energies opposite of those primary exertions from individuals. The positively aligned, tend to take in the same type of energy as source exertions. The neutral take in any energy and exert a synthesis of the negative and positive energies.

The Like-Minded: Unaffected by cosmic events, solely consisting of the physical and mental capacities.

Kamikaze: Highly charged individuals who use negative emotional signifiers to reduce their perceived survival rate, allowing the individual to free him/herself from the inhibition of fearing death, ironically, often ending in death. The kamikaze is a blueprint martyr.

The Generator of Collective Knowledge: The generators of collective knowledge occur at two levels: the mental-emotional and the spiritual. On the mental-emotional level the generators of collective knowledge are filmmakers, musicians, philosophers, scientists, and writers. These individuals create and devise new knowledge, new expressions, and expose society to their findings, advancing society in terms of our ability to conceive and understand.

The generators of collective knowledge in the spiritual realm devise and create new knowledge just as those mentioned in the paragraph above. The distinction between the two rests in the fact that the generators of collective knowledge in the spiritual realm disperse their information throughout the entire collective psychically. Another distinction is that the generators on the mental-emotional realm can be created, or create themselves, whereas generators in the spiritual realm are genetically or perhaps spiritually predisposed to carry out their function.

The Self-Preserving: The Self preserving are primarily confined to the physical and perhaps mental-emotional realms. Without the spiritual capacity to conceptualize of higher levels, the self-preserving look to maintain their means of survival with little consideration for the social unit, save personal gratification.

The Creation Myth

At the dawn of time, there was the essence of nothingness and the Edien, or, "one-essence." Edien grew slowly, and eventually filled the universal capacity. When there was no longer room for nothingness in the universal capacity, the Edien pushed outward in four directions. Though the Edien was and is a single force, through the distinction of distance in space, the Edien segregated into four distinct forces, characterized by their direction. Chaos emerged from the south, whereas its counterpart, order, emerged from the north. From the east sprang evil, and from the west its counterpart, good.

When these four distinct forces sprang into existence the universal plane manifested and the Edien attained consciousness, using the four essences as tools to measure distinction and reaction. The Edien, or, One-God—being part of both realms, and all distinctive forces in the universe—could not be all and control some simultaneously. So, in order to maintain balance, Edien created the universal God from the four distinct essences. Using the universal realm as a shell, the One-God confined the four essences and imbued the realm with consciousness.

The function of the Universal God was to maintain the balance between the four distinctive essences. But through loneliness perpetuated by consciousness, the universal God acquired a dual-purpose: one to maintain the balanced coexistence of the distinct energies, and one to satiate the needs of the four distinct essences confined within the universal shell. From this experience the Edien came to realize that consciousness, confined within any material form would acquire dual-purpose through consciousness: one to satiate balance, and one to satiate the self.

The first realm that the Universal God devised was the spiritual realm. While the Edien confined the four essences in one realm—the Universal God, knowing that if he imbued each of the four essences with consciousness he could be defeated[1]—stratified two essences into

---

[1] The One-God created the universal God. However, the One-God is simultaneously a part of the universal god. Therefore, the universal god can never overtake the One-God. However, if the universal god, a distinct and separate entity of the oneness, imbues the four separate

hierarchies, and imbued each lesser spirit with consciousness. Evil was processed and segregated into a hierarchy of demons, while good was segregated into a hierarchy of angels. Chaos and order were used to create free will, in which demons and angels could gravitate towards different options while remaining fixed to their disposition of essence.

While the universal god had created the manifestations of the four essences on the spiritual plane, he did so using the four essences derived from his universal realm. Due to this factor, the four essences of the one-realm manifested on the spiritual realm as well. While order manifested as the hierarchical order of the angels and demons, chaos manifested as the distinction between the two forces. Good manifested as virtue, and evil manifested as sin, both non-conscious entities. Because sin and virtue manifested, the demons were not only composed of evil, they were capable of committing it. As with all conscious entities, the demons had a dualistic purpose: to both preserve the balance of their realm, and to commit, or perpetuate, sin. The angels followed suit, in that they were composed of good, capable of acts of good, and compelled towards good as a result of dual purpose.

This is when the Edien realized that each world created below the universal would consist of increasing distinction. This is because the four essences manifest both in their natural form, and in the form they took on the plane directly above. In the instance above, the universal god used the energy from the essences in the universal realm to create angels, demons, a virtual free will, etc. In addition to these manifestations the natural form of the

energies he is composed of with consciousness, the four could thwart his position together and replace him.

essences on the one-plane manifested in the realm as well as sin, virtue, distinction, and hierarchy.

Creating the lower realms was the universal god's attempt to generate energy for his realm, and to spread among the spiritual inhabitants a raised consciousness, which would make them one with his consciousness, but still separate and distinct. The spirits however, were incapable of reaching a state of ascension beyond the spiritual realm, as they did not have true free will. Though the angels and demons could gravitate towards chaos and order, they were ultimately compelled to abide by their disposition of essence.

In order to allow isolated energy systems to reach a state of ascendance, the universal god devised a plan for the mental-emotional realm. This would provide conscious beings with free will. However, there is no survival mechanism drawing them forth, or helping them develop a sense of survival, pain and pleasure, which are the foundations of empathy. In other words, the beings would have free will, but they would have no sense of social obligation or collective existence.

The universal god then devised a plan for the physical realm. From this realm, man would develop a survival mechanism, would be able to become conscious of that which generates pain and pleasure. While the being would not have free will, and a highly-reduced state of consciousness, the survival mechanism would compel the individual towards survival, keeping the beings in seedling state from too great a harm or total self-initiated extinction.

When the being's mental-emotional capacities began to develop, and physical transformation followed suit, the beings would be able to reason, and would be imbued with awareness of free will. Then the beings had free will, social awareness, and if all went well, empathy, setting the stage for spiritual ascendance.

There was a spiritual uproar at this point. The angels believed that the resulting distinctions wrought on by progression down the realms would cause more distress than good. In addition, free will would give man the ability to elevate towards any of the four essences, meaning that spiritually ascendant beings of pure chaos, pure evil, pure order, and pure good, could be produced. This meant the potential for humans to overtake angels and demons. Many of the spiritual inhabitants believed the universal god was trying to replace them with a superior race.

To calm the distressed beings, the universal god promised that the angels and demons would have dominion over the humans, that they would help him maintain the balance while the humans were in their fledgling state. Some of the beings agreed. Those who did not, both a faction of angels and almost half the demons, were condemned and cast out of the spiritual realm into a segregated spiritual realm surrounded by the vortice of the physical plane. This is when the universal god realized that not only could he segregate energies within the fabrics of the lesser realms, he could segregate conscious entities within the fabrics of lesser realms as well. For example, he could segregate a spirit, such as a demon or angel, to an individual's body, or within the fabric of the plane's vortice.

The universal God went through with the creation of the mental-emotional and physical planes. He created the first humans, and was reluctant when he found that the essences of the mental-emotional realm had manifested in

24

the physical realm in the form of a tree. In addition, the essences of the spiritual realm had manifested on the physical realm as well, also in the form of a tree. The universal god told the humans not to go near these trees.

Several other manifestations occurred on the physical realm which the universal god did not expect. Of the minor manifestations there were: spirits, or, ghosts, conscious spiritual entities confined within the physical planar vortice, manifestations of the spiritual plane's good and evil.

The spiritual plane's chaos and order manifested on the physical realm as distinction and singularity. Distinction was a calculated refraction innate within the system of planar creation. In order for the total essence of a manifestation on a lesser realm to be less than the manifestation on levels above, the essences must disperse. For example, the manifestation of the universal essences exists within each living creature. The less living creatures, the more essence within each. Distinction causes dispersal of essence, which is important to maintaining the order of the hierarchy. In the event of distinction generation, singularity maintains the natural undistinguished, balanced state of the essences. Without singularity all manifestations of the essences would disperse. All independent systems would be equal in this instance, and all collectives would disperse and dissipate.

While the minor manifestations were many, there were only two primary manifestations of major consequence.

Collective Life

The first was the manifestation of virtue and order on the universal plane: collective life. The universal god found that collective life was life sustaining for mankind, which meant that mankind could survive, should it decide to abandon the universal god's sacred grounds.

Due to the dual composition, the collective life had two universal purposes: to sustain the life of the virtuous and serve as warning to the life of the sinful and destructive should it get out of hand. The second universal purpose was to sustain the life of the lesser beings, such as animals and plants.

The intrinsic purpose of the collective life was not to create, but to facilitate creation. It has performed its function unerringly since its inception, and it is for this reason—and the fact that the collective life is an inadvertent blueprint of the universal god's plan for achievement: isolated virtue and order—that the universal god is envious of the collective life.

Collective Death

The second inadvertent manifestation was collective death. Derived from, and a manifestation of, chaos and evil, collective death served two universal functions and one intrinsic function just as collective life.

The first universal function of collective death was to remove the excessively sinful, the excessively withdrawn, and the excessively virtuous from physical existence. Collective death achieved these means not only through decomposition, but through pestilence and virulence, byproducts of rot. Due to pestilence and virulence, collective death not only had the power to remove physical remains from earth, it had the power to convert organic flesh into dead tissue, giving collective death a limited, but powerful amount of choice in determining who and what met demise at the whim of the collective death.

The second universal function of collective death was to conceal the acts of the sinful and the evil against the virtuous. The collective death was to accomplish this not only on a minor social scale—by concealing the remains of murderers and infecting witnesses to sin—but also on a revolutionary scale, by concealing over time the dissolute cost of war.

The intrinsic function of collective death is to find a means to releasing those angels and demons confined within the physical planar vortice. Though this has yet to be accomplished, collective death played a role in the following scenario, which occurred not long after the inception of collective death and collective life:

At this time, one of the universal god's highest angels, now condemned to hell, changed form to work through a small crack in the physical realm's vortice. His intention was to come to the physical world, seduce the first woman, and have children with her. But when he arrived in the physical realm he found himself without powers, knew himself to be on sacred ground, and knew he could not change back.

The first woman crossed the fallen angel's path as she was sauntering, and he convinced her to eat the fruit of the tree, which was a manifestation of the mental-emotional plane. At the moment she ate the fruit, she prematurely ascended to the mental-emotional level. She then convinced the first man to eat of the fruit as well, and he too prematurely ascended to the mental-emotional level.

The universal god became angry, and abandoned the physical realm. This is not to say that he abandoned mankind. Rather, his presence in the physical realm was no longer felt. The universal god did not remove himself from the mental-emotional realm however. The universal god's primary conduit of communication ever since has been the mental-emotional realm, and the mind of mankind.

The Composition of Man

On each plane, man is composed of what we perceive to be dichotomy. At the physical level we have receptors, which help us perceive both pleasure and pain. At the mental-emotional level we have emotions that make us gravitate towards good or evil. At the spiritual level we use our faculties to spread or exemplify virtue or sin.

This dichotomy is essential to facilitate free will. In order for man to have the choice between various compositions, he must harbor the four essences and must be able to gravitate towards them equally. For this reason, man is composed of good, evil, order, and chaos. In this respect, we are not created in the physical image of god, but rather, the spiritual composition or "spiritual image."

We are brought into the world with an equal balance of the essences, four winds blowing in opposite directions simultaneously. From the first action we take, and the first reaction we make, our composition changes. Our compositions change due to several circumstances:

1. We take in energies from around our physical being and process them: In life, we have the choice to choose between good, evil, chaos and order. We also have the choice to immerse ourselves in the energies of other individuals. As we expose ourselves to, or segregate ourselves from, particular essences, we become increasingly composed of the essences surrounding.

2. We exert energies derived from our internal composition: When our soul becomes imbalanced, we exert the dominant energy into the world. The body ejects the dominant energy in order to re-establish balance, which in turn fills the spiritual collective with this energy. If enough people gravitate towards a particular essence, say, evil, this will upset the balance of the four essences in the spiritual realm. However, since man is a manifestation of the universal god both individually and collectively, there is generally a balance between the four essences. This is to say that, in the world there is a balance of individuals who gravitate towards the four directions. The most significant implication one can derive from this phenomenon is that, though mankind has free will, we are all likely born with an innate inclination towards one of the essences. The balance is consistent, and rarely deviates from equilibrium more than a minute amount.

3. We make decisions that increase our tendency towards or away from the physical survival mechanism: The more we are inclined towards the physical survival mechanism, the more likely we are to succumb to immoderate pleasure and gravitate towards sin and evil.

To avoid the negative repercussions of immoderation and immersion in sin, mankind must as a society develop a single set of moral and ethical principles. This will not only inhibit the current culture of sin, it is segue to spiritual ascendance.

Spiritual Ascendance

While the virtuous acknowledge that life is wrought with strife and pain, they believe immersion in each plane is essential to mankind's spiritual ascendance. The physical realm is essential because it allows a contained spiritual essence to grow and change largely independent of the surrounding environment. When we near the time of spiritual ascendance—according to the universal god's plan—there will be substantial levels of good within man and much evil in the world.

Traversing the mental-emotional realm is essential because on this plane mankind is imbued with free will, or, the essence of the One-God. Free will is the manifestation of the one-god. There can be no resistance to free will. We ultimately have no choice but to follow the will of the four winds and practice the greatest semblance of free will that we can. No action on this planet or in the entire universe goes against the grain of the One-God, and there is no possible resistance to the One-God.

The personal goal of mankind, according to the universal god's plan, is to freely choose to exhibit virtue. The universal goal of mankind is to act as a tool, through which the universal god may isolate systems of energy. These isolated systems have the potential to exhibit and reach a capacity of good. With the energy of the virtuous, the universal god hopes to create a kingdom in which he can re-create the planes in an isolated environment, and imbue man with the ability for spiritual ascendance, with free will and distinction, but without evil. Man will have choice, but in this new universe within a universe, evil will no longer exist. Deprivation of evil from mankind's repertoire of dismal choices in a chaotic and corrupted world will not be felt if the universal god's plan is achieved.

In order for mankind to fulfill their universal goal, they must undergo spiritual ascendance, in which the merits of virtue compel us towards good, because we have made the choice to condition ourselves as such. Doing so is the only way to ensure an autonomous society which preserves the moral and ethical rights of all individuals.

The virtue among each individual, while perpetuated by free will and choice, creates an order among the individuals. Each individual has reached equilibrium, in that they are not interfered with by any other individual, but at the same time, all individuals are working towards a synonymous goal. The society, therefore, reaches the preferred state of pure virtue coexisting with a balance in which pure chaos equals pure order.

Book II:
Philosophy of the Evil

Chapter I:
The Eleven Creeds

1. There is no spiritual ascendance. Mankind is already perfect. All actions are biologically and mentally justified responses.

2. Though there is no spiritual ascendance, the evil must ascend to a state in which the individual experiences freedom from all perpetuates and inhibitors of evil. By freeing oneself from these factors, the ascendant will better utilize these tools for the manipulation of others.

3. Servants of evil exhibit the qualities of the elements of evil and do not reach the ascended state. The servant is controlled by the elements of evil, whereas the ascendant controls the elements of evil by instilling them and augmenting them in others.

4. The universal purpose of the ascendant is to spread evil. Their intrinsic purpose is to create servants of evil. The ascendant creates servants from the pure, the innocent, and the lukewarm.

5. Purity is emptiness – The pure turn their heads away from sin, not to avoid corruption, but rather to avoid facing the absurdity of reality. To deprive oneself of the essences of evil is to deprive one of a part of our natural composition.

6. Purity is Blindness – The pure hope for justice, even if by sinful means. Those who wish for the death of

murderers are blind to the contradiction of their desires for justice. While the drive is innocent, their ignorance of sin and evil allows them to fall prey to their desires. Innocence is ignorance. Corruption is knowledge and fulfillment.

7. Lukewarm apathy is potential energy waiting to be summoned to a cause. The vehicles are pain, suffering, fear, despair, anger, hatred, envy, greed, lust, and sloth.

8. Pain, suffering, fear, and despair are known as limited elements because they all have the potential to inhibit and spread evil. These are the means to creating and controlling servants.

      The ascendant can cause these feelings in the servant of evil, but those exhibiting these elements of evil rarely spread them to others. They may increase their own composition of evil, or inhibit their potential for evil, however.

9. Anger, hatred, envy, greed, lust, and sloth spread evil. In addition, these elements of evil can be spread by individuals exhibiting the elements. For example, greed of one can lead to another's envy, which could lead to pursuit of lust from the loved ones of the greedy. Whether ascendant, like-minded, or servant, all individuals have the potential to exhibit and perpetuate these elements of evil. These are the absolute elements of evil.

10. There is only relative free will. We are servants by nature of a force greater than ourselves. We are prisoners of sin and virtue, pleasure and pain. The purpose of discourse between the sinful is to explore that of darkness

and sin which binds us so that we may become free from darkness, and then choose whether or not we want to reengage the system as a controller, as opposed to submitting from birth.

11. There is only one natural law: survival of the fittest. If we are strong, we have no need for deterrence. If we have no need for deterrence, then why should we abide by the laws prescribed that ensure our protection from others via deterrence?

Laws are a means of being civil, but what good is it to be falsely civil? If the intent and drive are apparent, then obviously there is a problem with deterrence. In this respect, the servant of evil is often more free than the servant of any of the other forces.

Chapter II:
The Elements of Evil

Each element of evil manifests as a dichotomy in which one end allows control over surroundings, and the other controls the individual. Therefore, attaining ascendance to the realm of sin requires moderation between the extremes of each element.

I. Pain and Suffering

Pain is not a manifestation of sin. Rather, pain provides us a means to interpreting our potential for survival on the physical level. As humans we are compelled to move away from pain, thereby increasing our chances for survival.

Upon emergence in the mental-emotional plane, man is imbued with consciousness. This is when—for the sake of society and the augmentation of man's perfection—man should make the choice to suffer.

Suffering is essential to the continuation of the human race. The universal goal of mankind is to suffer and perish in the wake of disease, finding moderate pleasure to quell our ailments, so as to facilitate to the growth and resistance of the future generations.

Mankind should thrive with the same resilience as viruses and bacteria. Their resilience is in part due to constant warfare with antibiotics and conventional medicine. As a result, there have been instances of bacterial super-strands and viruses impervious to conventional medicines.

By allowing and working in coordination with the evolution of viruses, we develop immunity to disease.

Likewise, mankind evolves resistance to emotional reactions to violence, or, desensitization through suffering.

Mankind's Predisposition toward Pain

I. Mankind will choose the absolute of pain over the uncertainty of pleasure: In most instances, mankind fears change over pain. When an animal operates solely on a primitive level, the being is compelled to move away from pain. But due to consciousness, mankind has the ability to qualify pain.

Though our ability to do so functions with accuracy, the human mind will, in balancing two sources of pain considering the variable time, choose the current source of pain, even if greater than the future potential for a reduction in, or lesser source of, pain.

Contentedness is the biggest distraction in our lives. The evil look upon those who strive for positive change with more respect than they look upon the content.

Even if contentedness means a constant of destruction or pain most will happily abide by its rules to see sameness, no probability of a changing future: battered wives remain with abusive husbands to maintain a family unit, or in hope that someday he will change, for example.

II. Pain as Ritual: the Departure from, and Return to, Ritual or Reinforced Pain: This phenomenon is best exemplified by warriors who, after war, feel as if they have no purpose and return to the painful state of war. Also includes individuals who return to a lifestyle whose primary or subordinate feature is pain.

III. Pain as an Extension of Pleasure: Pain as an extension of pleasure—the primary areas from which we derive pleasure being: ingestion, inhalation, sexual gratification—can cause at first weakening of the pleasure, and eventually can lead to pain. An example of pain as an extension of pleasure would be excessive dry sexual acts. The acts will cause chafing, dulling of the synapses in the genitals, and eventually potential discomfort.

IV. Pain as a Byproduct of Pleasure: Pain occurs as a byproduct of pleasure, variable to time. For example, some pain that is a byproduct of pleasure occurs simultaneously, such as can be the case with nicotine. There are other pains which occur after the acquisition of pleasure, such as is the case with a hangover.

Adaptations to Pain

The Masochist: The masochist is defined as any individual who has learned to receive gratification on the mental-emotional level from the infliction of physical pain upon him/herself by him/herself, or another individual. Masochistic tendencies are means to adapting to natural inclinations towards pain.

There are two forms of masochists: those who receive emotional pleasure from the pain, and those who use physical pain as a means of release from either guilt, or need for control. All provide means to emotional gratification.

However, the masochist is a benign, yet troublesome manifestation among the evil. Masochism is a perversion of our perceptual tools on the mental-emotional plane, and is best reserved for the slaves of the ascendant evil.

Do not learn to enjoy pain. Learn to withstand it. To enjoy pain is to acknowledge the fact that you use physical means to control your emotions. When we use the perceptual tools from a lesser plane to cope with problems on a higher level, this is known as **regressive coping**. Regressive coping is essential to maintaining the order of subordinate evil, but is poison to the ascendant evil. The poison should only be administered to slaves by the ascendant being. Others could potentially raise the likelihood of regressive coping by causing anguish, conflict, and confusion within the ascendant individual, but this would likely be in vain.

The Martyr: Martyrdom is a spiritual means of adapting to the pain of a society, or perhaps merely symbolizing it, through death. As with masochism, there are two forms of martyrdom: the intentional martyr, and the inadvertent martyr.

Intentional martyrs either sacrifice themselves to preserve what remains of their social unit (defensive martyrdom), or make a final stand against an aggressor, knowing death is imminent (aggressive martyrdom). The aggressive martyr takes the pain of his or her social unit and attempts to disperse it throughout the social unit's aggressors, like suicide bombers. Defensive martyrdom is an attempt to circumvent further pain to the martyr's social unit through self sacrifice

Inadvertent martyrs are individuals who are representative of a people and are killed in the line of their function. These martyrs generally fall under the category of defensive martyrdom, as the martyrs die while actively trying to circumvent further pain instilled upon their population. In many instances, the martyr dies due to their pursuit of preserving their society's remaining happiness.

In either and nearly any instance, the act of martyrdom is virtuous, but condoned by the evil, especially when martyrdom occurs among their servants.

Mankind's Predisposition toward Causing Suffering

Mankind's natural inclination towards destruction is the result of mankind's need for "total knowledge" of an object: the curious child deconstructs his or her toys to determine what makes them work, comes to realize the concept of irreversible change, the final aspect of existence: counter-existence, or, non-existence.

In addition to mankind's natural inclination towards destruction as a means to understanding, mankind has natural inclination towards destroying that which he does not understand, thus eradicating the source of fear of the unknown in mankind, as well as augmenting mankind's knowledge of this unknown.

While mankind's inclination toward destruction begins with an innate curiosity, the knowledge of irreversible change and potential non-existence, combined with aggressive and competitive survival instinct, leads us to mankind's greatest predisposition towards causing suffering and destruction: war.

In this respect, it could be argued that man does not have a predisposition towards causing suffering and destruction, but rather that man's search for self-betterment, and preservation of survival generally leads to the suffering and destruction of others, especially in instances where resources known culturally or instinctually to perpetuate life become limited. War, suffering, and destruction, therefore, are natural byproducts of man's will to survive, and are inherit in mankind's already-established perfection.

While it is true that the three natural byproducts of man's will to survive: war, suffering, and destruction, lead to non-existence of objects and functions, it is also true that if we understand an object or function completely through destruction of the object or function, then there is no longer any need to experience it.

Death therefore, is an essential process in the natural order. All things become stagnant. It is emotional attachment that causes us to wish to maintain things we enjoy.

Suffering as Punishment

Advocates of reform refute the notion of punishment. At the heart of their ideology rests the primary oath: mercy, above all things. But mercy is not reform. The very nature of the Edien is such that consequences are inevitable. This is because, while mercy is powerful, it rarely instructs, or alters function. Mercy provides a path for the forgiven to continue immoral action.

Mercy allows forgiveness without reform, without consequence. Punishment is forgiveness manifest as reform.

Torture: No servant of the ascendant evil, or of the highest orders of evil, should ever be tortured unwillingly. However, a good servant of evil wills himself to torture. The ascendant must keep their servants in order by implementing a means to perpetuating regressive coping within their servants.

Torture accomplishes this by reducing an individual to the edge of the **self-serving threshold.** The self-serving threshold refers to the point at which an individual will sacrifice all values—ideals, pride, emotional and physical attachments—in order to survive.

The self-serving threshold varies, and each individual sacrifices values in variable order. The selfless individual will generally sacrifice values in the following descending order: pride, physical attachments, ideals, emotional attachments, for example.

When in a state of torture we are reduced to the point at which contentedness has long since left scope of our perception. When tortured, people can sacrifice all physical gratifications and immediate emotional gratifications for the prospect of future retention of these gratifications. The prospect of gratification, or, hope, keeps us alive. This is why it is so essential for the ascendant to imbue their servants with a reasonable and acquirable hope.

Emotional Suffering: While fear and despair are considered independent of pain and suffering, they are essentially a form of emotional suffering, which means that many phenomena associated with pain and suffering are applicable to fear and despair. The distinctive qualities are discussed in the following two sections.

II: Fear

While pain is a means of measuring our survival on the physical level, fear is a means of measuring survival on the mental-emotional level. While we are not inclined towards fear, save in controlled instances, there are five types of naturally occurring fear and despair. As with pain, fear has the potential to be both a perpetuate and inhibitor of evil.

Natural Occurrences of Fear

Universal Fears: The fear of dying is the primary universal fear. Throughout life individuals create "controlled fears" in order to compensate for their fear of dying, which ultimately is the impending fear of the final proof that we are not in control.

Socialized and Inherited Fears: Most phobias fall into this category including fear of heights, fear of animals, etc. Individuals use these fears to develop their controlled fears. Someone with a fear of heights, for example, might develop a high from riding a roller coaster, or climbing mountains. Developing controlled fears, and pushing yourself to meet their limits, may lead to abolishment of the socialized or inherited fear.

Inherent Fear: Inherent fear consists of both universal fears and fears derived from socialization, possible inheritance, etc.

Controlled Fear: Controlled fears are those that we gain control over through conscious faculties.

Controlled fear can help lead an individual to ascendance. Transcending the boundaries we establish through controlled fear, we can eliminate our socialized and inherited fears.

Nightmares: Manifestations of evil on the mental-emotional realm, nightmares distort the work of dreams. While nightmares cause fear, they could almost be considered a controlled fear, or counterbalancing fear, as they are generated by an individual to quell guilt over an individual's perceived wrongdoings.

Nightmares are also a product of fear of the unknown. While nightmares produced as a result of perceived guilt are therapeutic, nightmares of the unknown are highly damaging, and are amplified manifestations of the actual fear one feels of the unknown during waking hours.

Delusional Fear: Delusional fears have the potential to either inhibit or perpetuate evil. Rarely, but in some instances, cults being a primary example, delusional fears spread delusional fears in others. Most often, delusional fear spreads destruction, or murder at one end of the spectrum, and pacifism at the other end of the spectrum.

There are two primary sources of delusional fear: self-infliction and power.

Self-Inflicted Fear

Self-inflicted delusional fear can be intentional or unintentional. In many instances the individual begins to ascribe to delusion as a means of coping with reality. In reality, when we are young we piece together the world, and we have fears of the unknown. For the delusional, a delusional reality begins to manifest, and the gaps within this delusional reality cause fear. In the event of delusional reality creation, most delusional fears are actually, from the standpoint of the delusional, very rational fears about encroaching reality.

Most other forms of self-inflicted delusional fear are merely rational fears produced by stimuli grounded in delusion. For example, jealousy or envy can lead to the delusional fear that your partner is committing adultery.

Reinforced Fear: There are three different sources of reinforced fear. As with delusional fear, there is self-inflicted reinforced fear. In addition there is natural socially inflicted reinforced fear, and manipulative socially inflicted reinforced fear.

Reinforced fear also has the potential to inhibit or spread evil. For example, deterrence is a socially reinforced fear. In either case, deterrence leads not to total inaction, but to a reduced amount of actions that are deemed unacceptable by a nation or conglomerate of individuals. On the other hand, fear of another country will cause individuals to murder and destroy just as delusional fear has the potential to.

The significance of reinforced fear is that it is all encompassing. Through manipulative socially inflicted reinforced fear, the ascendant can create and control delusional fear and controlled fear in another individual. By establishing and/or manipulating another's controlled fear, you can affect the degree to which their inherit fears effect them.

Self-Inflicted Reinforced Fear: Each individual has a different sensitivity to self-inflicted reinforcement, which is the degree to which a phenomenon or event reinforces the belief that some other phenomenon or event is going to, or will very soon, occur. The less reinforcement required to instill a principle or drive, the higher the sensitivity.

Other examples of self-inflicting reinforced fears are the fears of hurting another individual, hurting oneself, fear of conspiracy, fear of being voyeuristically exploited, etc. All of these fears, while reasonable, are often self-inflicted reinforced.

Though the above fears could be initiated by external circumstances, the conspirator fearing conspiracy, the exhibitionist fearing voyeurism, or, exhibition without their consent, regulation, or control, they are still internally reinforced. Only when an external source serves to reinforce a fear on a consistent basis, can it be referred to as a socially-inflicted reinforced fear.

Natural Socially-Inflicted Reinforced Fear: Socially-inflicted reinforced fear depends on natural, repeated occurrences to cause fear.

For example, if you wake up two days out of two weeks and the cable is out, or the car doesn't start, this doesn't mean your car will never start and cable will never work. Some resort to even more general reinforcements, that these phenomena are proof that life is horrible and everything goes wrong.

The media (manipulative socially inflicted reinforced fear) influence our fear of the social collective, and our virtual individual powerlessness against crime and warfare.

Manipulative Socially-Inflicted Reinforced Fear: Manipulative socially-reinforced fear uses social reinforcement to manipulate either delusional fears, or our natural fears.

III. Despair

Despair, as with fear, is a means of measuring our survival in the mental-emotional capacity. We are not naturally inclined, save in rare circumstances, towards pain and despair. However, we are inclined towards love, the central instrument that inadvertently spreads despair.

Despair is a measurement of relative dissatisfaction with a current state in life. Therefore, for relative dissatisfaction to occur, it generally must be preceded by a relative satisfaction. Despair is generally lament over loss of satisfactory circumstance.

There are those who idealize a perfect life, and a perfect future. From this ideal, an individual may derive a relative dissatisfaction with everything reality presents to them. These individuals have established a delusional threshold of satisfaction, and are chronically in a state of despair. In this respect, despair is also lament over a disparity between ideals, which manifest as delusional goals in a reality which cannot facilitate these ideals.

Love as Prerequisite to Despair: Since humans have natural inclinations towards love, they also inadvertently have natural inclinations towards the variable of despair. Each time the individual experiences loss of love, the residual despair creates reluctance towards returning to love. In this capacity, despair has the ability to extinguish the will to love in an individual. Likewise, love can extinguish despair.

Loss as a Prerequisite to Despair: Loss of objects acquired, of self-esteem contained, both result in despair. Loss brings us to a state of hopelessness, causing us to fear the potential for loss. If inactivity, or, stagnation, occurs, the individual's despair will become chronic, arising whenever action is contemplated. This cycle allows, or perhaps forces, despair to manifest as raw self-doubt. As with all forms of despair, despair over loss has the power to inhibit an individual's gravitation towards keys to ascendance: love, including self love, which ultimately is what we lose and lament during despair over loss, and love of perfection, or, love of idealization.

Idealization as a Prerequisite to Despair: Most individuals have the capacity to develop ideals, and derive from experience reasonable personal expectations for themselves and the world: a medium between idealization and the reality we're enmeshed with. Individuals incapable of this natural mediation between ideal and reality are met with chronic despair highly reminiscent of despair over loss of met expectations.

IV. The Absolute Elements

Carnal Sin: Under carnal sin falls hate, anger, envy, lust, greed, and any other sin that cause us in extremes to revoke or compromise the moral and ethical rights of others. The sins that compromise moral and ethical rights of others are called socially-inflicted sin. Sin without the motivation of sin, and you will be one step freer from consequence.

Hate & Anger: Hate is one of the most provocative sins, as it not only provides outlet for buildup of energy, but also the ability to spread sin to others. While envy and greed fall into the category of carnal sin with hate and anger, the latter of these elements requires only a will to the emotion or impulse itself.

For example, in order for greed to spread evil and sin among others, the greed must be accompanied by a will to succeed, and a general desensitization which allows greed to supersede empathy.

Hate however, requires only the will to hate. While envy and greed require an innate desensitization, hate provides emotional desensitization, increasing in direct proportion to the self-envelopment hate and anger causes.

In addition, while envy is partially defined by dislike of another individual or individual's circumstance, envy does not necessarily manifest as an aggression towards the source.

Hate, on the other hand, is an emotion that drives. While envy in itself is the only action resulting from envy, hate perpetuates further action to qualm our dislike of a source problem. In this respect, when envy drives an individual to take action, the envy has evolved into a form of hatred.

Envy: Envy, as lust, are qualified as carnal sins in that a carnal sin is defined in terms of its ability to sow hatred of others in the sinful individual, and hatred of the sinful in other individuals. While all sins have the potential to create hatred of others and towards others, only those most reactive to natural phenomena, spreading evil on a consistent basis, are qualified as carnal sins.

Lust: Lust shares many elemental qualities with envy. In terms of elemental stratification, lust precedes envy. Lust, as envy, share twofold elemental properties, as they perpetuate both intrinsic or self-inflicted evil and universal evil. While hatred has the potential to perpetuate intrinsic evil, the purpose of this intrinsic evil is to imbue the individual with the will to destroy a source that inspires hate.

Lust as a perpetuate of universal evil occurs when an individual allows lust to compel them towards action. If the action results in infidelity, and the resulting evils: envy, hatred, commodification of an individual, and greed of this commodification—then lust has succeeded in spreading universal evil.

Intrinsic lust works to pervert the mind. Even if lust does not compel an individual to action, it can often successfully compel an individual to thought, which is a distraction, and reinforcement of lust, which, if untended to, results in action.

Greed: Greed over another's assets is envy. Greed inspiring action over another's assets through the vehicle of hatred is war. Greed of sex is a manifestation of lust. Greed is the all encompassing carnal sin, as greed has the potential to manifest as each of the carnal sins.

Self-Inflicted Sin: The self-inflicted sins are: sloth, gluttony, and in some instances lust and envy. The self-inflicted sins are defined in terms of consequence. The self-inflicted sins are the most apparent of the elements of evil, as their consequences manifest more rapidly than other sins, and the mannerisms and physiology of the individual are characterized by the very sin.

Sloth: Sloth is basic inaction. The causes of sloth are: apathy, physical impediment such as obesity, obsession, and fear. While the sloth may disgust those around him, generally, the sloth only inflicts harm or hatred upon the self.

Gluttony: Gluttony paves the way for one form of sloth. Gluttony also paves the way for self-hatred and disgust of those surrounding you. Gluttony leads to isolation, fear, and delusion in extreme cases. Overindulgence of any form malnourishes the mind and the spirit.

Pride: Pride inflicts damage on others, reinforces delusion, and affects surrounding individuals dependent on the dynamic of power between the prideful and society. The prideful in power draws his men into vain battle, causing anguish among his people. The prideful without power leads the prideful to envy.

The lower the prideful individual's power the higher the likelihood of pride to cause envy, the higher the prideful individual's power the higher the likelihood that the pride will result in evil spreading through the society in the form of envy, doubt, hatred, etc.

V. Absolute Inhibitors

Pain, suffering, fear, and despair have the potential to be both perpetuates and inhibitors of evil. In addition to these limited elements, there are the absolute inhibitors of evil: guilt, love, and the virtues.

Guilt and love are qualified as autonomous inhibitors, as they naturally compel individuals. The virtues, however, must be consciously implemented. This is where the primary distinction between the autonomous inhibitors and the virtues lies.

Autonomous Inhibitors

Guilt: Guilt is powerful because it is chronic and can stop reinforced sin and takes much less conditioning. Guilt is not a virtue, as virtue is chosen. Guilt is innate, generally natural to the human condition. Guilt compels the individual not to perform sin.

In the event of spiritual ascendance, as posited by the virtuous, guilt may no longer be necessary, as empathy replaces guilt. Empathy precedes guilt because empathy has a greater capacity to prevent an act of sin, whereas guilt is a consequence of sin, inhibiting the likelihood of future sins.

Love: Love is distinguishable from the virtues because, as guilt, love is preconditioned in mankind. Unlike guilt, which compels an individual to not perform sin, love has a tendency to compel an individual to perform good. In other words, at guilt's worst, it produces apathy and stagnation over sin whereas at love's worst, an individual is still compelled towards good.

The distinction between love and love lost has to be made. Love lost leads to despair, possibly envy and despair. Love, when attained, when maintained, is an absolute inhibitor of evil, with the rare exception of those who love evil, and perpetuate evil and augment their composition of evil through the vehicle love.

The Virtues

The primary distinction between the virtues and the autonomous inhibitors is that virtues are consciously implemented, whereas love and guilt are autonomous. There are five virtues which work to counter the several elements of evil.

The virtues are harder to perpetuate, as man must make the decision to do so, whereas with evil we merely "choose not to choose" and let our inhibitions take us. While sin will arise as a result of apathy, virtue rarely, if ever, does.

Temperance: Temperance counters gluttony, greed, lust or any of the excesses. Temperance is the primary virtue above all virtues, save hope. From temperance the remaining virtues spring naturally. Moderation of excesses in greed requires charity. Moderation of excesses in pride requires humility. Moderation of sloth requires diligence. Moderation of lust requires chastity, and moderation of gluttony and other excesses requires abstinence. Temperance, therefore, is equal gravitation towards sin and virtue, as a foundation from which virtues can be more clearly measured by the conscience of man.

Charity: Charity counters greed in the self, and has the power to counter envy in others. Charity is also known as generosity.

Chastity: Chastity counters lust. Chastity is the conscious decision to abstain from sexual "temptations".

Abstinence: Abstinence counters gluttony and all excesses.

Humility: Humility counters pride in the self, and hatred and envy of those in our immediate influence.

Diligence: Diligence counters sloth, and commands the respect of others. It a diligent man carries out virtuous functions, he may instill hope in an individual or society.

Hope: Hope is a unique virtue, an extreme that absolves the extreme of our bodies and minds telling us we are to perish. When the survival scale on the physical and mental-emotional planes veer towards death, hope can pull us out of this, and creates in the imagination, a relative ideal survival to counter submission to death.

Chapter III:
Distinctions in Evil

Hierarchy of Evil

Universal Evil: Like death, universal evil affects people without predisposition. The universal realm consists of one conscious being: the universal god.

Spiritual Evil: The spiritual realm consists of not only several conscious beings, but several species. The most significant of the spiritual planes' conscious species are demons and the essence of nightmares.

Nightmares

The essence of nightmares, sometimes referred to as Baku, is a single conscious entity which feeds off of guilt. Ironically enough, nightmares appear to share a, for lack of a better term, symbiotic (or symethereal, to coin a term) relationship with man, meaning they share a beneficial spiritual or ethereal bond. When mankind sleeps, the essence of nightmare enters the mental-emotional plane through the dreaming. The essence becomes refracted and isolated in the individual minds of man, as each man has an ethereal capacity that prohibits the essence from fully entering a single mind. The consciousness of the ethereal substance remains in the spiritual realm, so the essence of nightmare isolated in man merely reacts with guilt to produce our "nightmares". These nightmares often manifest as benign fear-instilling compensations for guilt. In a sense, the nightmare, produced equally by man and the essence, is self-inflicted punishment for an individual's guilt. When the individual wakes, they relent over the nightmare, or feel relieved of their return to the waking. The isolated essences then return to the spiritual realm, providing nourishment for the conscious essence of nightmares.

Demons

The demons of the spiritual realm, the few that remain, exist within the confine of a complex hierarchy, and are compelled to both their universal and intrinsic purposes. While demons perpetuate evil by various means, one particular means is by manipulating the essence of nightmare, their nature compels them to do so, and therefore, they are unaccountable for their acts, thus, immune to consequence of sin.

Of the demons that remain, only two manifest on the physical or mental-emotional with a frequency that allows mankind knowledge of their presence.

Baal: Idol of fear in nightmares, perverts dreams, creates guilt through dreams rather than absolving it. Though guilt is an inhibitor of evil, the proper balance of guilt, counter-drive, and conflict will cause insanity, an unstable state in which mankind is rarely accountable for their actions, which are generally evil.

Andras: Andras is the overseer of demonic alchemy of manipulation. Instilling broken hope is one of his specialties. In entering the minds of mankind, he finds disparity between the dreams of two individuals, and instills hope, sometimes administering the proper mix to create an obsession that will deter one and further provoke the other.

Causing insanity by administering the proper balance of human emotions, physical drives, and conscious conflicts is known as the Demonic Alchemy of Manipulation. While humans can practice this, and the ascendant is the closest to the demonic alchemy of manipulation we will come, humans cannot acquire the ability of administering human emotion, physical drive, and conflict demons do.

When Andras was created, he was born predisposed to the knowledge of mankind's future existence. In his knowledge he found that there were twelve elements in man capable of manipulation: the five emotions, the five senses, the two dream essences, nightmare and dream.

When God proposed the creation of man the condemned despaired and Andras rejoiced. He coaxed most of the demons remaining to stay and hone his precious science in the hopes that someday the universal god would imbue them with the ability to ascend to the universal realm upon proving man's ascendance futile.

Variations in Evil

Mental-Emotional Evil: Man is imbued with consciousness, allowing him to choose to be evil, and therefore making him accountable for committing sin. In order for accountability to take place, the universal god created consequence to inhabit the realm with consciousness. Both consciousness and consequence are autonomous entities.

There are few conscious inhabitants on the mental-emotional level, perhaps to leave room for the consciousness of mankind to inhabit. Nightmares occasionally dwell in the mental-emotional plane, but they are hardly considered evil. Rather, they are beneficial to the ascendance of mankind.

Some nightmares aren't properly retrieved when an individual wakes, and these tiny, unconscious essences of nightmare dwell aimlessly through the mental-emotional. So far the phenomenon has no negative impact on the consciousness of man, nor on the realm itself.

Physical Evil: Physical evil consists of two distinct forms: the physical drives we choose to indulge when our conscience tells us otherwise, called intrinsic evil, and the physical manifestations of evil in the world outside of man.

Intrinsic Evil: Before mankind was imbued with consciousness, the physical drives that compelled us were by no means evil. Now that we are able to choose between what we know to be good and evil, it is still not the drive that is a sin. It is allowing ourselves to be compelled which is a sin. Still, we must recognize the physical drives as a counterpart to sin now that we are conscious beings.

Intrinsic evil also consists of the natural essence of evil within us. Because the essence is isolated within our physical "shell" it is contained in the physical realm and contributes to the total capacity of evil on the physical realm.

Intrinsic evil is the most common way to indulge servants. Physically gratify, emotionally destroy, become their ailment, and they are your servants truly.

Affiliations with Evil:
Chaos and Order

Though evil, chaos, and order are distinctive forces, through man they form conglomerates. All evil manifest in man is affiliated with either chaos or order. Consequently, ideals of autonomy and revolution in the evil are derived from their chaotic or order-based alignment.

Chaotic-Evil: The creed of the chaotic evil is as follows:

True evil cannot be defined by calculated action, especially revenge. Selective destruction is composed of order. There is no place for order in true evil. Nor will chaos follow the order of what man considers evil. When chaos and evil are one, we have reached the point of truth.

The only moral to abide by is our own. Then the individual order of each man will create the greatest evil of all: universal chaos, a violent autonomy.

The reigning champion of this era will be collective death. Composed of our very essence, collective death will recognize us as spiritual brethren, and rather than being forced into battle as the entity has been in the past, we shall willingly join in his next endeavor, which is to release havoc upon earth by unleashing the evil contained within the outer vortice. Only then can pure chaos be achieved, which will foster the growth of a violent dynamic of survival of the fittest, causing unanimity of violence and evil in a world where virtually all else is variable.

Order-Based Evil: The creed of the order-based evil is as follows:

Order is crucial to the maintenance of evil. Chaotic evil nearly resembles insanity. Can the chaotic evil in a world uninhibited by order be considered true evil, or is it merely repercussive action that mankind cannot truly be held accountable for?

In order for evil to spread, there must be order. There must be stratification, a distinction between the ascendant and the servant, between the servants of evil and the servants of good. The chaotic evil concern themselves with pure chaos. What of pure evil? The only way to spread pure evil is to distinguish between that which is and is not pure evil, and eradicate the negating capacity. This is our only means to a dynamic in which all individuals choose either evil or servitude to the ascendant evil.

Chaos as a means to perpetuating a new order of evil. Delusion as a means of causing breakdown and dispersal of current power. The remaining power vacuum is the means to our new order. That is the creed of the evil order-based sect.

Contact Information:

If you are interested in acquiring further information on the works of Henry Kirchhoff or Psychoplasmic Pulp Press, please contact us:

psychoplasmicpulppress@gmail.com

www.ingramcontent.com/pod-product-compliance
Lightning Source LLC
Chambersburg PA
CBHW060538030426
42337CB00021B/4321